Blackbird
and the
Mirror

I0164563

Cheryl Loudermelt

Copyright © Cheryl Loudermelt 2018
www.cloudermelt.com

All rights reserved. No part of this publication may be reproduced, distributed, or transmitted in any form or by any means, including photocopying, recording, or other electronic or mechanical methods, without the prior written permission of the publisher, except in the case of brief quotations embodied in critical reviews and certain other noncommercial uses permitted by copyright law. For permission requests, write to the publisher at the address below or email resources@idyllowl.com

Idyll Owl Books
875 S. Estrella Pkwy #6882
Goodyear, AZ 85338
www.idyllowl.com

Published by Idyll Owl Books 2018

ISBN: 978-1-949089-00-4 (Paperback)
        978-1-949089-01-1 (eBook)

For those I love
and lovely strangers
who unknowingly inspired
this book.

Blackbird
and the
Mirror

Portraits

Watching

People are at their
best when they think
no one is . . .

but always
    someone
    watches now

    like that girl
who lets her coffee
get cold while she
tries . . .
    to capture
the essence of herself
    on her phone.

If she wanted people
to know her, she would
      stop
taking pictures
of perfect skin
and show them
    the face of her soul

    blissful sin
as she takes
the first bite of a cookie
she spent . . .
    five
        full
            minutes
trying not to buy.

In The Plane

Hoped he wouldn't be
my neighbor,
    my butch barricade
    blocking the aisle.

Six hours, close proximity,
not a word about that rough elbow.
Half-smoked no smoking signs
    drive him to twitch.

Three small bottles
of his whiskey
clink in the cart.

This is the wagon train.
The flight attendant is Cookie,
    and he's the trail boss
looking out for lost cattle.

There's a brush fire
    underneath
his eyebrows, like Brillo,
    and his smile,
a nervous rattler under grass.

Hope he finds a sunset
    to ride into,
    a cigarette,
    and a light
the moment we land.

Hours of an Hour

matte paint on a tattered fence
    she talks about nothing

    lights another cigarette
    passive suicide
can't even see the smoke
against the sky

imagine that it hangs
    as lifeless as the
    conversation
that it spreads
thin as butter

there is no magic
I have no words
    say nothing
nod and stare

she talks about nothing
hope she feels
I am listening
    hope she feels
    anything at all

Cheryl Loudermelt

Jump Shot

Flight is windless,
        effortless.

He's a heron swooping
over a river of broken asphalt.

Wings, strong and wide,
        raise in praise
to the god of hoop dreams,
fall with a caw and swish,
an answered three-point prayer.

Cares, blossoms,
        float away
from muscular branches
taut trunk,
and land
near faded high-top shoes.

Soles pull apart
    and show his socks
every time he moves.

Ice Queen

arctic words, a
    harsh
yet . . . fragile
sheet of glass

    so thin to hide
    the pain
inside
    her snowcapped
    paragraph

cycle swords hang
from her gaze
frost reflects
    in her eyes

I think
    I saw
        a penguin
passing by

Changing Shape

he is every bit a moth
those not-quite butterflies
metamorphosis alters
by the moon

he speaks with his hands
because his mouth is blind

always trying to find
lost words he never had

not so graceful, but
determined to dance in the porch light
or campfire flames he can't touch
      for burning
   but fans
with stubby satin wings

Garden

When the air is light
and carries the fragrance
    of wet potting soil,
she remembers her garden.

The pumpkin vines
    overran the watermelon
and choked out the tomatoes.
Sunflowers stretched against
the wind as high as her window.

She watered every day,
even when it rained,
but never tasted
a single strawberry.

Dragon Lady

her scales are
made of diamond
like
    she sparkles
but will cut deep

she wears black
and jeans
years of routine
camouflage

no makeup
    no fuss
except a little paint
to hide the bits as they
    get gray

always tired
    always worn
always there
at all hours
impossible to break

but don't be fooled
she is a dragon
    made of diamonds
sitting on a hoard
of unworn shoes

Cleopatra Eyes

half a pound of black kohl
draped
    like silk curtains
    in a light breeze

    sixty-year old
innocence

she wears a funny hat
with an ensemble that
doesn't match and one
    dangly
        rhinestone
    earring

Barflies

As low down
as a man can get,
he'll smoke your
last cigarette.

Fuzzy black hair,
A patch on his chest.
He's like a teddy bear
others want
     to choke to death.

Tatted up tough,
one says "Mom,"
the other is a bull
     . . . I think to warn
people what he's full of.

Yesterday, he was
an Army Ranger, Hell's Angel,
     a widow
     and a father of four.

But here, beers on tap and
faces never change.
Everyone knows what he isn't,
except him.

Kicking his boots beneath the bar,
he waits for drinks,
     like his stories,
no one buys.

Disappearing Act

the girl holding that
cigarette is a mystery
    to herself
    and to me

cup laced with
Chantilly cyanide
    but she knocks
    it down smooth

high melon ball
low well shooter
generic brand vodka
    tonic

nothing to cure
her sense of style

chiffon chemise
half size too small
    exacerbating
every lump and line

she vanishes
in smoke she
    pushes out
through her nose

Inheritance

Shoes from a stiff collared man,
open hand at a back door, arches
    reserved
for those who fill plates
and pews.

Jeans from an uncle,
    circa '78,
a few holes, only
at his armpit swamps and
    gnarled knees,
with a smatter of
ancient grease.

    He got his aunt's hands,
fingers swan feathers
in concrete.

    His grandfather's hair,
cow-licked above his eye
and crawling beasts.

Grandma's spine
twisted beneath
elephant skin.

His father's temper,
abrupt fluidity,
and his sense of rhythm
        from his mother's heartbeat.

He got a few minutes to tap his feet,
a bus pass from the city,
a breath of shade
        and sleep.

But others come,
        always others,
a woman
and a girl who got her mother's eyes
        . . . and whispered orders
        not to stare
at the man who lets them
take his seat.

Inconvenient Store

shoulders sticky
   like honey
but she's no bee charmer

hair thick and stringy
must've mistaken hair gel
and petroleum jelly

she looks like
she doesn't care
and bemoans
      -loudly-
to the clerk that she
      -misplaced-
her last pair of clean underwear

. . . and her car's in the shop
   her dog's at the vet
   her kids are at school
   man's down at tent city
for drinking behind the wheel
. . . but never mind . . .

she's just in for a quickie
a large Mountain Dew
   chocolate
and a cigarette for after

Time Capsule

a spool of shiny
    yellow thread
a strip of Scottish tartan
rusty steel key
    from a tattered gun box
    a war long forgotten
an angry letter
and a drop of blood
saved inside the hem
    of an old hanky

a roll of silver duct tape
because it was supposed
to fix everything

she thinks that doing this
will keep everything he is
    immortal
in wool and string

but she buries herself
more than she buries him
because he will think of her no more
and someday
    she'll dig him up again

Star Crossed

One minute he's blasting
laser cannons.
An epic battle, a crash,
hurling down, then
. . . darkness, and it's over.

Opens his eyes, but
doesn't know where
he's been all night,
or that he was a hero
     minutes ago.

Can't remember a
dream or melody, but
hums at the sun
streaming through
lines of plastic blinds.

Thoughts in pieces,
          clinging rings
          around Saturn,
          dry lips,
mounds of Mercury.

. . . but this is Earth.
Of that much, he's certain,
because she's in his arms,
in his bed, with her head
on his chest and her hair
an orange nebula sprawling
across their space.

In the morning,
he blinks away
stardust.

Dancers

they've got history
    it's it in the lines
around her eyes and
in those loose strands
    turning gray

but she lets him lead her
even knowing he may
    cause wrinkles

his hand soft on her waist
backward slowly on the floor
    sideways through time
she thought was lost
    until the music stops

and now
    she must forget again
just when
    she was near to letting go

Blackbird and the Mirror

She'll never be the same,
split ends, hair unbrushed,
unwashed. Every inch,
    ashen skin . . .
her blush rushed past.

She was a blackbird,
but little girls, they say,
      suck away
their mother's color.

Baby blackbird, little thief
sleeps under wing.
Perfect, peaceful,
almost never cries.
Flawless like mother was
      once . . .

Blackbird never laments
flying tattered and unflattered.
She sees reflected only
the best of her feathers.

She thinks
she holds a mirror,
      not a child.

The Elephant Walk

longed for those
    commercial breaks
from the piano
fingers on the keys
playing the only game
         we knew

press a key
      perfect pitch
he was never wrong
at least about music

from his pea colored recliner
he flipped through channels
    king of his control

    finally
he'd find nothing
but ads and jingles

      and lumber
to the piano
yellow toenails
clicking on cheap linoleum
bald head spotted with age

he'd play for me, Mancini
The Baby Elephant Walk
    only on the break
    between
one sad story and the next

together for a moment
in the lightness
of that song
playful as we never were

but the song ends
   . . . all songs do

and he rose up from the bench
said nothing, wouldn't or couldn't
without music underneath

left me there to plunk away
    while he walked away
       like the elephant

Little Tweet

doesn't know the song
she makes up as she goes
feathers fly, frolic
and she is dancing

dancing,
          dancing . . .

the music stops
and she trades silliness
for stillness

because grandpa
has lost his feathers
but she knows
     by instinct
the notes and beats
that light her feet
came down to her
         from him

so little tweet
lifts up her beak
for a peck on his
withered cheek

sings him a song
she makes up as she goes

inside
     he is dancing

Stronger Than Steel

The kind of canvas
that pays the artist,
inked like a brutal comic.

His black cap flipped back
        fails to hide
Eiffel Tower eyes,
steel on the inside;
        they grow sharper
as people draw close.

Even his cheek scruff
looks gruff enough
to grate parmesan.

Imprisoned in that t-shirt
        muscles rattle
the bars of their too small
        cotton cage.

He feathers his son's hair
        to the side,
dabs away some catsup
on the boy's chin
and lands his arm gentle
        on the boy's shoulders.

A hummingbird thankful
        to the dogwood branch
for a sturdy place to land.

How to Make a Man

take a boy
tell him not to cry

then break his heart
a half dozen times and
tell him to be strong

feed him
spaghetti on Tuesday
leftovers on Friday
a beer on Saturday
       and Sunday
make him mow.

he's done
when worry lines
carve little
       canyons
around his eyes
and strands of snow
twist through his beard

but still
let him bake
a few more years

How to Make a Boy

take a man
and let him ride
    a parking lot sea
captain on the back
of a grocery cart

watch him
as he finds a quarter
on the sidewalk and
    dips to pick it up

let him admire
        a rainbow
        in the arc
of a water hose

give him
new jeans to spoil
        and a dog
to roll with in
        the wet grass

never scold
        smile
and kiss his nose

Soldier On

Once he marched,
now he learns to crawl.

Sixty year old child
seeing his family
for the first time.

Get to know the wife again,
          forgotten son,
a new treasured friend,
and grandkids.

Thank you,
hard to utter,
          hard to aim.

He claims he's proud
even of the things
he'd rather not see
          in rewind.

A grouch to hide
the tender spot he missed
while hardening the rest.

All people speak,
they say in whispers.

. . . hero
    . . . don't you know?
man saved lives
. . . grand firefight . . .
    . . . medals?
            yes . . .
they gave him plenty.

Now his days are
    filled with concern
over the right length of sock
to wear with sneakers and
scheduling his golf game
        before his body heals
from the last eighteen.

And his nights,
good whiskey cures
        . . . almost everything.

Grumpy Old Man

Maybe he'd be happier
    if he was clean.

Under his nails,
engine grease, and
who knows how much
ham sandwich.

An annoyance only
comparable to a pebble
    in the work boots
he's already worked through.

Every day, rinse, repeat,
and a long drive home.
Can't be bothered with
the extra effort of shampoo.

      Kiss at the door,
spot on the sofa,
two plates for dinner,
favorite show, and
        time for bed.

A blanket of yesterday's sweat,
a pillow of today's stiff spine,
    and sheets murky
with tomorrow's mortgage.

The Wolf and Granny

Hair starts at his forehead
    and disappears
(sort of) behind
the veil of a white tank top.

It reappears and covers
his arms, like paint
to his knuckles.

He's made
primarily of fur
and muscles.

    This and that
    from the cart
is no trouble at all.

In her wheelchair,
    granny sighs.
He asks, "you all right?"
She says she's tired.

And he promises her
a favorite dinner
and a foot rub.

Pays for her things,
while she dreams
    of later,
the wolf's hands
swallowing her feet.

Angel

six months along
and she still won't
remove
that belly ring
    straining
against her pregnant outie

never could stop
slurping down those cigarettes
tank top squeezing her sections

bra straps showing
    of course a different color
than they should be

she is the height of white-trash fashion
yet she wrangles that little boy
    like a rodeo clown
    and the big one too
that calls himself her husband

The Waitress

always the best
at serving the worst food

she plops into the teal booth
belly bouncing the beverages
    takes an order
never uses a pen
    but always perfect

a son at home
she scrapes a life
    from ones and fives
but mostly ones . . .

never dreary
    never droll
        wishing the best
while she restocks the sugar
    and knows
    every customer by name

getting twenty percent
        is a good day
        but so is giving
a hundred and ten

At Reception

silver nails clack
    on glossy wax
    pretty grain
    of cherry wood
finished early

but that clock
. . . is slow

twelve stories up
her eyes on the window
        counting
the rainbow of cars
      passing by

. . . time creeps
      but minds fly

soon she'll be curled
in a hot bath with
bubble froth

won't think or clack
      until she goes
back tomorrow

Meticulous

stacking envelopes
-return send-
-return send-

every one is full of promise
and the vicarious rush
of watching her child
go further. . .
-return
                send-

arthritic knots
      bird feet fingers
pain but no complaint

send-
                -return
send-

stick on another stamp
          and hope
                  send-
for the best for the one
she loves most
to fly where she thinks
she failed . . .

send-
      send-
            never return

Days Like This

She shoves the car door
        -open-
but it slams again.

Woke up
        spitting anthrax.

Climbs out, heels crunch,
        dress tear, and
        shiny, toothy
people everywhere.

Hello, she claims, but thinks
        . . . without the –o.
People are like papercuts.
The sky opens.

Across her face,
        brisk burst of rain,
a flash of something . . .
flush of fire, a glow,
        . . . a quiver
quick forgotten.

        Like youth,
her pink umbrella,
the keys in the ignition

the crack in the window
letting in the rain.

Standing in the Storm

so much rain inside his hurricane
    so cold inside December's cloud
now a flash that strikes and fades
    steady never ending rain

wrath of life in every sculpted line
cold like death so he believes
the spark so brief
    but blinding
followed too close
    with dark and damp

the angry cloud
tears petals
from the flower

wind
    carries
        away

so rage and crash sweet hurricane
cold carves weakness from the tree
lightning blinds and burns debris

        the underbrush
      once cleared
    reveals the soil
and rain makes fertile ground

Carving Pumpkin

Life goes on.
Sometimes that's the worst thing,
and red hair plastered
to tears like glue.

Red flush, swollen
jack-'o-lantern face
twisted, shived
    guts nearby,
and a hollow place.

Still, the night will pass,
    even when it shouldn't.
        even when
the world should wait . . .

There's still light inside,
flickering November.

All hallowed eve . . .
in warm red ember.

She lived as she was
    in the pumpkin patch.
She lived as she was
    on the fence post
as the children frolicked by
costumed in the dark.

She'll live in rich cinnamon,
new shape, new taste,
and life goes on.
Sometimes,
that's the worst thing.

Going to See Grandma

She presses her face against the glass,
drinks the green and gold leaves,
counts cows gnawing the fields,
follows the river crawling
          between trees,
gasps each purple flower
or violent bloom.
All things childlike and fragrant.

She presses her face against her hands,
shield against mundane.
Music thumping black and chill,
heels pounding drum and angst.
     Dark eye shadow,
     hair a purple flower,
     violent bloom.
All things known and misery.

She presses her face against the sky.
     Lips pour grateful honey
for the Sunday that saves her
every time she makes the drive
     from normal life.
Yard full, flush with flowers,
that fade, wait, and bloom.
All things lush, sweet familiar.

And each time
    she presses her body in,
for the smell of cherry almond hand lotion,
black coffee, and clothes dried on the line.
Young pink flesh mesh with old and gray,
that mingling moment the only thing
about her that has never changed.

All things fragile, except stone,
    granite. Overgrown,
violent bloom each year
    of purple flowers.
She wanders the path well-trod.
Memory warm in graying flesh,
flat within arms of green,
She presses her face against the grass.

Beginning

This is not the end.
    Beside the bed,
    she watches
her own heart beat in
green and out of rhythm,
but this is not the end.

They come in flocks
to say goodbye, but she
won't say that word.
This is not the end.

Alone in the room,
she smooths sparse
white and wishes for a
mirror, but doesn't ask,
because this
    is not the end.

She'll dream of all she
hasn't done and measure
regret in spoons full of pudding.
This cannot be . . .

The end.
Something whines a siren song
and she hears tears, please, pleas,
    and finally,
slips on her shoes, sneaks away
laughing to watch the scene
unfold from the door.
This is not the end.

Afterlife

I hope you found your field of reeds.
Your heart was light enough
for fields of wheat and paths
    to walk forever with the gods.

Your heart was light enough.
Elysium must have called you
    to walk forever with the gods
    to curl in the stars to dream.

Elysium must have called you,
or did Valkyries lift you to Valhalla
    to curl in the stars and dream
to feel only joy and feast?

Did Valkyries lift you to Valhalla?
    I hope you found your field of reeds,
somewhere you cannot feel my grief.
    I hope you found your field of reeds.

Cheryl Loudermelt

Aftermath

didn't know him
except by what he
left behind

a trove
of broken
glass like diamonds
in the road

swept aside
and later swept
away

A Haunting

in the stairwell and
       hovering
in high windows
he never looks up

doesn't wonder
    why the pictures
       move
    sometimes

doesn't question
the thin footprints
in the carpet

long strands of black and gray
that cling to his socks
and clog the shower drain

the hangers rock from
nimble invisible fingers

he never looks up
but she manifests
      hope

     a ghost
who believes
what once was love
will live again

Cheryl Loudermelt

Flowers on the Mountain

We rose wild,
        seeking sun leaking
through the canopy,

grew the same roots,
        deep like stubborn weeds
cluttering the perfect green.

Drinking up the melting frost,
we danced with rain, and deer
and wind in spring-
        waltzed
to cricket songs, laughed at fall,
as other flowers shriveled off.

But winter plucks us
        one-by-one,
stifled by the snow.

Our petals shed,
        our withered leaves
an ache mountain flowers know.

Those gone before
succumbed with grace,
Their fragrance sojourns on the air,
and when it comes time
        to hide
my fronds in winter's fountain,
        I hope to fade,
        then remain
with the flowers on the mountain.

And we will meet again
        in spring
when all is fresh and white and green.

Born again, where we rose wild,
we will meet again in spring.

About the Author

Cheryl is originally from the Blue Ridge Mountains in North Carolina and Tennessee, but now resides in Phoenix, Arizona where she teaches English, listens to Chopin, and sings loudly when no one is looking, except her pet rats. She loves zombie history and anything made with salted caramel.

www.cloudermelt.com

Hummingbird

Cheryl Loudermelt

Whenever she told the story of him, she talked about the hummingbird. The tiny green bird laid motionless in the gray hallway of their apartment, so easy to enter, but difficult to leave. It had grown exhausted throwing itself against the glass, unable to reach the water or the sky. Three years into their marriage, she was beginning to understand exactly how the little bird felt.

For her, there was nothing really wrong except a constant feeling of fatigue. She had grown tired of making pots of black coffee, picking up soda cans accumulating on the floor, and staring at garbage he didn't take out in time for trash pick up on Thursdays. Later had become the tiresome refrain of their lives. Can I do it later? I'm too tired right now. Later, things will get better. Later . . .

If they had come home an hour later, the hummingbird probably would have died. It stared at them listlessly through shiny black eyes, too close to death to be afraid of their approach or his touch.

She could no longer touch him without feeling a sense of dreary endlessness, always the same, always lacking in real connection, but expected and habitual. She expected nothing better, not even later.

He touched her like he wasn't afraid to break her, as though she were an elephant, coarse, callous, and with hide thick enough to withstand anything, his mood swings, financial stress, illness. She carted it around, feet grinding into dirty hardwood floors that she didn't have the energy to clean, or the hope of keeping clean if she found the energy. He loaded her up and led her through dry grass, promising a drink somewhere across the wilderness, later.

But he touched the hummingbird gently, as though it were made of porcelain instead of flesh and feathers. It lay in his palm, unafraid of being crushed by his fingers, seemingly no more concerned than it had been on the floor. The hummingbird knew that location was unlikely to change the outcome. Maybe it thought the end was inevitable either way. Space and distance made no difference.

She felt lonely with him, as though he was miles away, thinking of something else, something dark. She stopped thinking, because wildfire spread rapidly in dry grass. Sometimes, she thought, to die would be not much different than living.

"Go upstairs. Mix some sugar into water in a cup."

She marveled at the bird he clutched so tenderly, the bloom of viridian against his pale hand, and she measured his merit by the kindness he showed a dying animal. No other man would take such care for a creature that meant nothing to him, and in that moment, she loved him. She had gone to fetch the water.

She did everything he asked, everything he didn't, and he did nothing but sit for days at a time, watching movies, reading the news, his laptop glued to his hands. She would get up and play fetch, even if she had to stop what she was doing in the process, school, music, family, friends, and sometimes life, because it started to be that when he spoke, her heart stopped, and not the way it had when he tilted the hummingbird's beak into sugar water.

That moment of compassion, of complete love, she had told the story many times to extol the man he was. Whenever someone would ask her why she stayed, why she carried on, she said it was because he was a man with enough merciful caring in his spirit that he nursed the hummingbird back to life for no reason other than love.

And he deserved that too, didn't he? Someone to try and pick him up off the gray floor, and dip him in sugar water, and hold him and try to make him whole again.

The little bird drank and drank, until he finally pulled the cup away and placed it in her hands. They went outside together, and he gently tossed the bird into the air. It didn't need a moment to adjust; it remembered how to fly.

He would never hold her gently and stroke her bright wings, or fill her beak with sweetness. When she put her arms around him that last time, she hugged him for the hummingbird, and when she let him go, she did so because he was the sort of person who would do everything for a hummingbird, and leave the woman that loved him for another time, for later, forever.

The hummingbird zoomed back for a moment as if to say goodbye. It was so close, she could hear the furious buzzing of green wings before it burst into the sky.

www.ingramcontent.com/pod-product-compliance
Lightning Source LLC
Chambersburg PA
CBHW060538030426
42337CB00021B/4320